**COMPACT
CYMRU**

C000296932

JONK at

~75~73

Editor: Myrddin ap Dafydd

Gwasg Carreg Gwalch

First published in 2017

© publication: Gwasg Carreg Gwalch 2017

ISBN: 978-1-84524-258-9
Cover design: Eleri Owen
Map: Alison Davies
Published by Gwasg Carreg Gwalch,
12 Iard yr Orsaf, Llanrwst, Wales LL26 0EH
tel: 01492 642031
email: llanrwst@carreg-gwalch.com
website: www.carreg-gwalch.com

Acknowledgements

The publishers wish to acknowledge their gratitude for these images:
© Images: Crown copyright (2016) Visit Wales

Fading lights on Llyn Gwynant

Contents

Introduction	6	Flora	42
The heart of the mountains	6	Rocks and minerals	44
Prehistoric settlers	9	Sygun Copper Mine	48
Roman roads	12	Slate quarrying	52
King Arthur's Cave	14	The Quarry Hospital	62
Dinas Emrys	16	National Slate Museum	66
Saints of the Celtic Church	20	Llanberis	72
Beddgelert church	24	Beddgelert	76
Sant Garmon's church, Betws Garmon	26	Capel Curig	80
Princes and castles	28	A Snowdon Car Journey	84
Snowdon's lakes	32	Mountain Guides and early travellers	92
Llyn Padarn	32	The Snowdon Horseshoe	94
Llyn Peris	32	Snowdon Railway	100
Llynnau Mymbyr	36	Padarn Railway	106
Llyn Gwynant	37	Welsh Highland	110
Llyn Dinas	38	Mountaineering	112
Llyn y Gadair	39	Electricity	118
Llyn Cwellyn	40	Tourism & attractions	124
Llyn Llydaw	40		
Glaslyn	40		
Llyn Du'r Arddu	40		

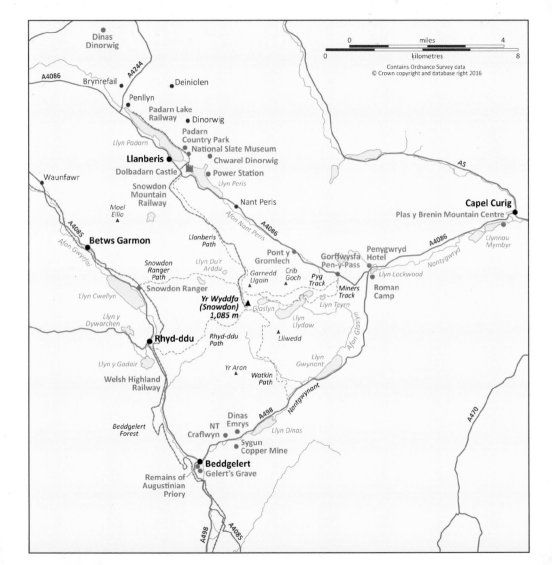

The heart of the mountains

In the heart of the ancient mountains of Snowdonia (*Eryri*), an array of leisure activities await the holidaymaker. This is one of Wales' main tourist areas, attracting fans from all over Europe and beyond. As well as the natural, scenic attractions of the area, it has a wealth of heritage and culture to offer. The Romans were here in their time, and legends of ancient Welsh heroes are associated with many a peak, lake and crag. The industrial heritage of the area is extremely interesting from both a visual and social perspective.

Previous page: Nant Peris and Pen-y-pass;
Below: Daybreak on a wintry scene at Llynnau Mymbyr;
Opposite: Crib Nantlle

Prehistoric settlers

Even in the remotest corries of the highlands and on the lakes of Snowdon (*Yr Wyddfa*), we will always be in the company of seagulls. Wales' highest mountain is just a few kilometres from the its beaches – as the crow flies. And it was from the sea and the coast that the first settlers came.

There are few extant remains of these early inhabitants, but on maps the words *carnedd* (cairn) and *cromlech* (burial chamber) can often be seen in the foothills. The oldest dwellings in the area are the huts which were home to the indigenous peoples of the Bronze Age right up until the Middle Ages. These early houses consisted of low circular stone walls with a conical wooden frame supporting a straw or reed thatch. Several such dwellings have been reconstructed in museums throughout Wales such as at the St Fagan National History Museum, Melin Llynnon windmill (Anglesey) and Castell Henllys (Pembrokeshire).

1. *Dinas Dinorwig; 2. 'Cytiau Gwyddelod'; 3. Dinas Emrys*

In the parish of Llanddeiniolen, near Llanberis, is the site of a fortified village which was one of the area's main defences, Dinas Dinorwig. The walls at the entrance are 4.6 metres thick, and deep ditches surround a hill above the Seiont valley. It is a prominent location within sight of several other Celtic forts along the north Wales coast, Tre'r Ceiri, Dinas Dinlle, Penmaenmawr, the Great Orme and Holyhead. The Celts settled from 500 BC, building a considerable number of hill forts, which even today remind us of the fortified hill-top villages of southern France, Italy and Spain. '*Dinas*' was the Celtic word for a hill fort (in modern Welsh it means 'city'), and there are several examples in the area such as Dinas Tŷ Du which occupies a splendid defensive position to the west of Llanberis; Dinas Mot and Dinas y Gromlech at Nant Peris and Dinas Emrys near Beddgelert.

Of all the different cultures which have come to the mountains of Snowdonia, it is the Celtic influence which is still most strongly felt. The Welsh language spoken here today derives from the language of the ancient Brythonic Celts who used to inhabit Dinas Dinorwig and the round huts which are to be found along the hillsides.

The way of life here has changed several times since then, and yet much of the Celtic imagination still survives here and the old Celtic legends have been passed on from generation to generation.

Several legends have grown in an attempt to explain some of the more unusual rock formations in the vicinity. At the bottom of the Llanberis pass is the bridge called Pont y Gromlech where there is a place to park cars beside three enormous boulders. This, according to the legend, is the old *cromlech*, where Celtic heroes were buried and when there was talk of blowing them up to build a road, there was such an outcry from local people that the authorities were obliged to alter their plan and create a bed for the road between the *cromlech* and the river.

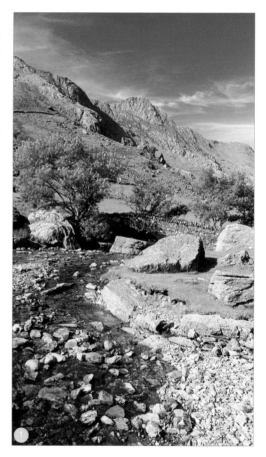

1. Nant Peris; 2. Y Gromlech

Roman roads

Driving roads through the mountains has presented challenges to engineers over the centuries and Nant Peris and Bwlch Llanberis were to remain exceptionally remote until some two hundred years ago. No one managed to build a modern road through the pass until the beginning of 19th century.

But the Romans had no such problems. Their main fortress in north-western Wales was at Segontium on the edge of modern-day Caernarfon and they had a temporary fort at Penygwryd, near the present-day reservoir.

One of the greatest contributions made by the Romans to Wales was a road network over the hills and mountains connecting different regions and forts with each other. Some of these must already have existed, but it was the Romans' methods of paving which made road travel so much easier. One of these was named after a Brythonic princess – Elen of Caernarfon, who married a Roman official, and Sarn Elen (*Elen's road*) was the name of the main road which connected northern Wales with the south through the Snowdonia heartland and the Cambrian mountains.

1. Llanberis Pass; 2. Gorffwysfa Peris at Pen-y-pass; 3. Penygwryd, at the site of the Roman fort

King Arthur's Cave

The mist descends rapidly sometimes in these narrow valleys and it's not surprising that stories of giants and fairies (*tylwyth teg*) abound. The longest rock climb in Wales is to be found beneath Bwlch y Saethau on the cliffs of Lliwedd, ascending a sheer 400m rock face. According to legend, it is here that King Arthur and the Knights of the Round Table lie sleeping, awaiting the call for them to save Wales once more from her enemies. There are many Arthurian legends in Wales – the historical Arthur was one of the predominant classic warrior figures in early Welsh poetry. He was the leader of the Brythonic Celts in a kingdom comprising southern Scotland, Cumbria and Yorkshire, the west of England, Devon and Cornwall and, of course, Wales.

The political equilibrium in the island of Britain was shattered with the departure of the Roman legions as their empire began to disintegrate around 400 AD. In the west the Irish invaded Gwynedd and Teutonic tribes came from the Low Countries, Denmark and Germany to eastern England. The Brythons united under King Arthur and his horsemen at the end of the 5th century and, by all accounts, he defeated the Saxons on twelve occasions and maintained the eastern borders of Wales much further than they are today.

Wales is full of legends extolling the feats and strength of their heroic king, one of which is located here above Llanberis. At one time the whole land was being blighted by an angry giant called Rhita. Several brave men fought against him but perished. Rhita would then remove their beards and add them to his flowing, if rather hairy, cloak. Eventually, there was just one hole left in the cloak which required a king's beard – no less – to fill it. A challenge was issued to Arthur, the most powerful king in the world at that time. Arthur came to the foot of the mountain with his army. To avoid suffering among his own men, Arthur himself accepted the challenge to fight the giant. The dreadful din of mortal combat resounded in the mists that lay over the mountain filling the soldiers encamped below with dread. Eventually, Arthur came down the

Bwlch y Saethau, between Snowdon summit and Lliwedd, under ice and snow

mountainside victorious. The giant's body was left at the summit. Each and every one of his soldiers climbed the mountain and slapped down a rock on the giant's body, and that is how the highest mountain in Wales was formed – Gwyddfa Rhita Gawr ('the burial mound of Rhita Gawr').

Dinas Emrys

Dinas Emrys commands a strategic position in the valley of Nantgwynant, one of the principal routes through Snowdonia. Rocky, steep and covered in deciduous trees, there is now a safe path, starting from Craflwyn car park (NT) to Dinas Emrys' summit above Llyn Dinas near Beddgelert. It is as natural a fortress as one could find, 250 ft (76 metres) above the floor of the Glaslyn river valley. There are some stone ramparts remaining of the Iron Age hillfort that once stood here and the base of a keep tower possibly erected by the princes of Gwynedd in the 11th century. Excavations in 1910 and 1954–56 revealed several periods of habitation at the site and discovered that there was a pool within the enclosure. A medieval cistern supplied valuable fresh water to the hillfort's inhabitants. The pool connects with the Welsh legend of the king, the castle and the dragons.

It was here that the Brythonic king Vortigern (*Gwrtheyrn*) came to seek oblivion following his treacherous deal with the Saxons in south-eastern Britain in 449 AD. He began to build a castle, but after each day's work was done the walls would fall during the night. This went on for some time before, eventually, his wise men told him to find a fair-haired youth who had not been fathered. He was then to sprinkle the boy's blood on the castle site. A young boy called Myrddin Emrys was found with the necessary qualification and taken to the hill-top for the ceremony. Upon being told the reason for his death he told Vortigern that the wise men were mistaken and that he would show him the truth. Myrddin led Vortigern to the base of the hill and into a concealed cave that led deep into the hillside. At the far end there was a lake in which a stone chest contained a red dragon and a white dragon. (These were symbolic representations of the Brythonic and Saxon nations.) He then told him that each night the two dragons awoke and fought each other and it was the tremors from this conflict that undermined the walls. He said that eventually the red dragon (Brythonic/Welsh) would kill the white one (Saxon) and it would be then – when the hill stopped shaking – that the castle could be built. The truth of Myrddin's

1

2 Twr Tower

Seston Cistern

Rhagfuriau Ramparts

3

words came to be realized and the wise men were subsequently put to death and buried in the field to the west of the hill. Myrddin had established himself as a seer and his future was secure; Vortigern, unhappily was pursued to the Llŷn peninsula (Nant Gwrtheyrn) and finally to his death.

The most conspicuous object currently on the hill is the base of a rectangular tower. It is generally accepted that this is part of an undocumented castle built by the princes of Gwynedd in the 11th century to guard the road to the mountain pass of Snowdon. In 1201 Llywelyn granted the Nantgwynant valley, including Dinas Emrys, to the Cistersian monks of Aberconwy abbey.

Dinas Emrys
1. *The summit; 2. Medieval remains;*
3. *The legend of the two dragons;*
4. *Looking down on Dinas Emrys*

Saints of the Celtic Church

The two lakes on the floor of the valley are named after two saints from the age of the Celtic Church: Sant Peris and Sant Padarn (*Sant* = Saint). Llyn Peris is the higher of the two lakes and above it stands Nant Peris and the ancient church of Sant Peris. This was the area's first social centre. During a later period, the focal point for the local populace moved to the new village of Llanberis, named, yet again, after the old saint of the parish. The village of Llanberis stands on the shores of Llyn Padarn and not those of Llyn Peris!

When Christianity reached Wales, it was upheld by monks and saints – as opposed to the episcopal institutions prevalent in the Church of Rome. Nevertheless, the Celtic Church was recognised by Rome long before Austin was sent as a missionary to the 'island of the Saxon tribes' in England. The emphasis of the Celtic Church was on a simple way of life and the establishment of small *llannau* (sing. *llan*, lit. an enclosed piece of land) in locations which were often remote. One of these saints was Peris. Not a great deal is known about him other than that his feast day would be celebrated on 11th December. Sant Padarn established a tiny chapel at Llwyn Padarn between Electric Mountain (*Mynydd Gwefru*) and the Victoria Hotel in Llanberis.

The saints would roam the land, visiting other *llannau* and spreading the Word. Sant Peris seems to have been quite a traveller as the old name for Bwlch Llanberis was Gorffwysfa Peris (*gorffwysfa* = resting place) – Gorffwysfa is the name of the hostel at the head of the pass to this day. Opposite the church in Nant Peris is the old well associated with the saint, in the garden of Tŷ'r Ffynnon (*well house*). Some of the walls around the well still remain, but, at one time, the whole well was housed in a small building a couple of metres high, with a circular seat set above the water. A pair of trout used to be kept in the well, a fresh pair being introduced on their demise. Lovers would go to the well and the sight of both fish together was deemed to be a good omen for them.

1. *Ffynnon Peris – the well of the saint;*
2. *& 3. The church at Nant Peris*

Originally, the church of Sant Peris was typical of several old churches in Wales – a simple, rectangular building. But a north and south transept were added in the 16th century and two chapels in the 17th century resulting in its unique shape. The most striking feature of the church is the chancel screen dating from the early 1500s. Its design is simple, but rather beautiful, and perfect for its setting nestling in the mountains. To the left of the opening in the screen there is a wooden community chest with three locks on it. This is known as Cyff Peris (*cyff* = chest) and probably dates from the 17th century.

There are several interesting tombstones in the graveyard: one of which relates the sad tale of a little seven year old boy called John Closs who got lost on the mountain in December 1808 and died in a snowstorm. The large church of Sant Padarn today stands in the middle of Llanberis – the present building dating from the Victorian era.

Nant Peris church

Beddgelert church

At St Mary's Church in Beddgelert, an earlier building is incorporated into the structure and it is likely that there could have been a cell on the site in the 6th century.

Within the Celtic tradition there was a strong monastic element. The princes and gentry of the area endowed monasteries, and by the end of the 11th century the monastery was built of stone. It had become an Augustinian Priory, a resting place for pilgrims on their way to Bardsey Island, in fact the Priory at Beddgelert was one of the oldest in northern Wales, except for the foundation at Bardsey. The north wall of the building is all we see today incorporated as part of St Mary's Church. The Charter of 1286 refers to the Priory as 'The House of the Blessed Mary at Beddgelert'. The present church was restored in 1880 and has beautiful stained glass windows.

St Mary's Well was to be found near the Royal Goat Hotel. The monks claimed that they could work miraculous cures with its curative waters. There is no trace of it today.

Bishop Anian, in the 13th century, wrote of the Priory that 'the house of the Blessed Mary in Eryri... is the senior religious house in all Wales with the exception of Bardsey, the Isle of Saints'. It probably was of Celtic foundation. Anian mentions its hospitality to the poor and to travellers and pilgrims.

All the early charters and chronicles of the Priory were destroyed in a fire that took place in 1283. Before that date Owain Gwynedd, in 1137, gave land to the house and Llywelyn Fawr added to its endowments. It was in his time, in the early part of the 13th century, that the earliest portions of the present church were erected.

The fire evidently did not destroy the church, though the roof may have been burnt. Bishop Anian begged Edward I, to rebuild the Priory. This he did, but there is now no trace of his work, as the last remains of the conventual buildings were pulled down in 1830.

The earliest portions of the church consist of the east and north walls and, probably, the lower part of the south wall of the chancel, which, however, has been increased in thickness externally. The features remaining in these walls are the

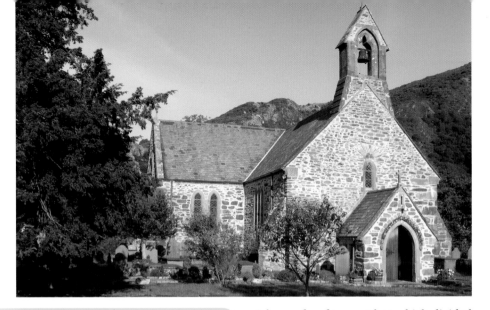

Beddgelert church

magnificent eastern triplet, possibly the finest architectural feature in the whole of Snowdonia, with two orders of chamfer all round, in Anglesey gritstone, brought, as tradition tells us, in small boats up to Aberglaslyn.

In the east and south walls are sundry recesses, shown on our plan, and on the north wall is the old priest's door from the vestry, which latter appears from an old print to have been of two stories. The very rich arcade of two arches which divided the Lady Chapel from the canon's choir is still intact and is the most elaborate in Snowdonia.

The monastic buildings were to the south of the church. In the later periods we know that Bardsey, Penmon, Beddgelert and Ynystudwal had become houses of the Augustinian Order. There is a tradition that at the time of the suppression great opposition was offered to the Commissioners, ending in fighting and bloodshed.

Sant Garmon's church, Betws Garmon

Garmon's name is sometimes connected with Germanus, the Bishop of Auxerre who was sent by Rome in the 5th century to preach against certain doctrines upheld by the Celtic church. Others maintain that he was a Celtic saint and many churches in rural and hill valleys in Wales are dedicated to him.

St Garmon's church is located on level ground in a low rubblestone-walled rectangular churchyard used, and extended, as a cemetery, on the north side of the A4085. It is a small mid-19th-century church built to replace a medieval church. It was built in 1841-2 in a simplified Romanesque style to designs of George Alexander.

The church has been rebuilt in a different position from the old one, as may be seen from the positions of the gravestones, the west end of the old church being apparently where the present chancel is, and the whole building pointing away from the road more to the north of east than to the south, like the present building. The only remnant of the old church appears to be the font, round the top of which is inscribed 'CAPEL : SANT : GARMON : BETWS : 1634', with a small four-leaved flower between 'CAPEL' and the date. There are no old trees in the churchyard.

St Garmon's Well is situated high up on Moel Smyddo, the hill nearly opposite the west end of the church and nearly a mile away. It is said to have occupied the position of the rude intake formed to supply water to the dwellings below.

Two or three hundred yards lower down the hill, towards the church, are the remains of a small structure, facing east, bearing every indication of being those of an ancient chapel. The doorway is in the north wall. The general construction would suggest an early 16th-century building.

Princes and castles

The main court of the princes of Gwynedd was at Aberffraw on Anglesey (*Ynys Môn*), but by the 13th century they also had another important court at the foothills of their natural fortress of Snowdonia at Abergwyngregyn. They also built castles in the highland valleys at Dolbadarn and Dolwyddelan. This strong line of rulers controlled north-western Wales and often led the rulers of the other regions of Wales in their resistance to Saxon and Norman rule.

The old name for Dolbadarn castle near Llanberis was Caer Peris, and it was subsequently called Castell Padarn. This is probably one of the oldest fortified defences in Wales – in the 6th century there was a fort here believed to have been given as a gift to Caradog, king of Cornwall, who brought an army to Wales to help Maelgwn Gwynedd defeat the English.

The existing castle was built around 1208 by Llywelyn Fawr to defend the route through the Llanberis pass. In contrast to Dolwyddelan castle, Dolbadarn has a round tower in the Norman style, and its romantic setting, with the crags of Snowdonia as a backdrop, has attracted artists for centuries.

Llywelyn Fawr was soon succeeded by Llywelyn ap Gruffudd. His road to kingship was a rocky one. In order to keep Gwynedd united, he was obliged, in 1255, to fight against his brothers, Owain and Dafydd, on the battlefield at Bryn Derwin above Clynnog. He captured Owain and imprisoned him in Dolbadarn castle until 1277. Llywelyn acquired the homage of all the Welsh lords – and even the English crown – assuming the title of *Tywysog Cymru* (Prince of Wales) for the first time ever. Edward I was not one to keep his word, however, and when he got his second wind, he spent enormous sums of money raising huge armies to invade Wales. Llywelyn was killed in an ambush at Cilmeri near Builth (*Llanfair-ym-Muallt*) in 1282 where a memorial stone refers to him as *Ein Llyw Olaf* – our last prince.

Dolbadarn was the final refuge of the last of the independent princes of Gwynedd. Dafydd, Llywelyn's brother, took advantage of its powerful location in 1283, before being forced to escape into

Dolbadarn castle

the mountains, where he was captured and eventually barbarically executed on the streets of Shrewsbury.

Edward I drew up plans for a chain of castles along the shores of Snowdonia – powerful strongholds which could be supplied from the sea. He had no desire to maintain mountain castles such as Dolbadarn and Dolwyddelan – they were castles to protect the lands of the indigenous people. Caernarfon, Conwy and the rest of the Norman castles were built to serve the oppressors.

At the time of the Glyndŵr rebellion, Owain Glyndŵr's arch-enemy – Lord Grey – was imprisoned at Dolbadarn. The castle returned to Welsh hands in 1488 when a lease was procured by Maredudd ap Ieuan. It became part of the Faenol Estate in 1627 coming into public ownership in 1941. Nowadays, it is Cadw, the organisation responsible for historical monuments in Wales, which preserves its history.

Dolbadarn castle in its mountain fortress

Snowdon's lakes

Snowdonia is renowned for the splendour of its lakes – on valley floors, their waters constantly reflecting the beauty of the surrounding mountains and also in the high cymoedd, there are several lakes which gleam like pearls in the shadow of the crags and they too are well worth a visit.

Llyn Padarn

A long narrow lake, 93 ft (28.65 metres) in depth at its deepest point. This is one of only three lakes in Snowdonia which contain *torgoch* (a native fish) as a natural species – some of them weighing over 450 gm each. A local fishing club also stocks the lake with unfarmed trout. Rowing and canoeing are popular on the lake as well as trips on a pleasure boat from Padarn Country Park (*Parc Gwledig Padarn*). The rowing competitions for the 1958 Olympics were held on Llyn Padarn and an annual swimming competition also takes place here.

Llyn Peris

On the shores of Llyn Peris in 1974 work begun on the largest pump-storage scheme in Europe. A network of tunnels were drilled through the mountain of Elidir Fawr so that the water could be released at short notice from Marchlyn Mawr to generate electricity through turbines embedded in the core of the mountain. Some 4283 hl of water flows every second producing 1,300 megawatts of electricity in 10 seconds. The water is stored in Llyn Peris during the day and then at night is pumped back up the mountainside to Marchlyn Mawr while there is off-peak electricity available. Special steps were taken to protect the environment and, surprisingly enough, every species of fish has found its way back to the lake, despite it not having being restocked.

1. Llyn Padarn in the mist; 2. Llyn Peris; 3. Llyn Padarn in winter

1. Padarn and Peris, with Dinorwig Quarry on the right; 2. Llyn Llydaw from the summit of Snowdon

Llynnau Mymbyr

This is a 'double lake' near Capel Curig and is one of the most photogenic in Wales with Snowdon, Carnedd Ugain, Crib Goch and Lliwedd (the famous 'horseshoe') as its dramatic backdrop.

Llyn Gwynant

This valley floor lake is up to 50 ft (15.24 metres) deep and contains trout. Above the north shore near the upper end, an old level was cut in search of copper but came to nothing – it goes in about 10 yards (9.14 metres) into the mountain rock. According to the early Welsh Triads, Medrod and Iddog held one of the three most treacherous meetings on these shores – plotting the downfall of King Arthur.

Llyn Dinas

A relatively shallow lake but visited by sea trout and salmon due to the size of Afon Glaslyn from here to the sea. There are two boat houses on the north shore and the remains of an older one can be seen on the southern shore.

Llyn y Gadair

Cadair is Welsh for 'seat' or 'throne' and the rocky hillock on the south-western shore was known by this name – legend having it as the seat of a golden haired water beast. The Gwyrfai path now offers easy access to the marshy shores.

Llyn Cwellyn

The deepest lake in Snowdonia – 122 ft (37.18 metres). The 13 ft (3.96 metres) dam was built in 1976 to add to the water supply needed for the Caernarfon district. The overhanging precipice that dominates the north-western shore is called Castell Cidwm (*cidwm* = wolf) and legend places a fort on its summit although no trace has ever been found of it.

Llyn Llydaw

This is a sheltered location at the foot of Snowdon. In contemplating its quiet waters, it will come as no surprise that Llyn Llydaw at 58.5 m is one of Snowdonia's deepest lakes The remains of an old Celtic *crannog* have been found here – a village built on an island of wooden poles, using the water of the lake as a natural defence. The path from Gorffwysfa, crosses a causeway over the lake – when this was being built for the copper ore mill in 1853, an old log boat was discovered in the mud.

Glaslyn

A circular lake under the buttresses of Snowdon. A tale is told of an exceptionally strong – and bearded – woman who lived in this cwm – Cadi Cwm Glas. When one of the miners began to make fun of her because of her profusion of facial hair, Cadi held the unfortunate individual by his ankles over one of the leats running into the copper mill! There are also many legends and stories about fairies associated with this lake.

Llyn Du'r Arddu

Du (black/dark) is the predominant colour of the waters of this lake which is at the base of a cliff, Clogwyn Du'r Arddu, one of the most renowned rock faces in Wales for climbers.

Flora

Over the centuries the variety of plants and flowers in Snowdonia has attracted many naturalists.

Welsh folk literature and memory go back to the time of the Celtic druids and many traditional herbal remedies have been passed on from generation to generation. Identifying and studying the local flora was part of our heritage and there would be skilled herbalists in every neighbourhood. The first recorded visit by a herbalist from outside the area was Thomas Johnson, an apothecary from London who came here in the company of Thomas Glyn, Glynllifon in August 1639. Although that was not really the best month for finding alpine plants, Johnson recorded in his journal that he collected a significant number of the rare plants for which Snowdonia was famed.

From a Welsh perspective, however, the most influential naturalist to visit the area on several occasions was Edward Llwyd (1660–1709). Hans Sloan, the President of the Royal Society, referred to him as 'the best naturalist in Europe at present', and he is considered to be one of

the most versatile Welshmen ever – he was a scholar, a naturalist, an archaeologist, and a traveller.

At the top of the Welsh botanical charts is Lili'r Wyddfa/Snowdon Lilly (*Lloydia serotina*), a small insignificant little plant with thin reedy leaves and white flowers with a green stripe along each petal. It only flowers for a short time

1. Edward Llwyd; 2. Snowdon Lilly (Lloydia serotina)

– about a fortnight at the beginning of June. The plant was discovered by Edward Llwyd in 1690, and was named in Latin in his honour. This is the rarest alpine plant on the island of Britain and is only to be found in some five or six locations in Snowdonia.

During the Victorian era, ferns became a great source of interest and consequently botanists began swarming over the rocks of Snowdonia in search of them. The tragedy is that several species of rare fern were taken from their natural habitat to gardens and greenhouses over the border. Some species were totally wiped out while only a few specimens of others were left on inaccessible cliffs beyond the clutches of collectors.

Despite these losses, conservation is now the watchword, and if the rarest plants are out of reach, there are plenty of other specimens to attract and amaze the naturalists who come here. There is probably no other area like it throughout the island of Britain and the remarkable botany of Snowdonia is a subject which could fill any number of volumes. The observant rambler is sure to find several unusual specimens on the most accessible tracks, but the lesson, hopefully, has now been learnt – in order to continue to enjoy them, none of these plants should ever be lifted.

Rocks and minerals

Today there are very few obvious remains to draw visitors' attention to the importance of copper mining in Snowdonia. Nevertheless, several generations ago, it was a major industry. There are still some traces to be seen, however – old shafts on the hillsides, the disused barracks and mills as well as a few odd bits of machinery. The presence of copper ore in the rock is what gives the clear blue-green hue to some of the lakes in the area. The name 'Glaslyn' for example, literally means 'blue/green lake'.

One of the earliest mines above Nant Peris employed between 40 and 50 men. As you walk towards the summit of Snowdon from Bwlch Gorffwysfa (Pen-y-pass), one option is to follow the Miners' Track. This goes past the old workers' barracks at Llyn Teyrn, the copper mill at Llyn Llydaw and ascends to the old workings at Glaslyn which are almost six hundred metres above sea level. It is difficult to imagine the deafening cacophany of blasting and milling which would have filled the air among these crags some two hundred years ago. Buckets on a wire ropeway and tramways would bring the ore down from the mountain.

The working conditions, of course, were very arduous in this type of terrain. Only during the summer months was it possible to work some of the highest shafts such as those at Clogwyn Coch near Llyn Du'r Arddu. During the hardest months, the miners would get an extra blanket in the barracks! The winter of 1801 was exceptionally hard when a tunnel had to be cut through the snow to reach the level, as the drifts were some 18 metres deep in places. Women and children were employed in the mill to break the ore with hammers before it was taken to ships from Swansea moored at Caernarfon.

The journey from Bwlch Gorffwysfa along the A4086 down to the harbour is easy enough these days – but that was not the case two centuries ago. The Caernarfon road came to an end at the big rock in Cwm y Glo and there was nothing for it but to use ponies along the mountain track – Lôn Clegir – or else take a boat along the lakes to Nant Peris. As was the

1. Copper rubble, Llyn Llydaw;
2. Old copper mine; 3. Llyn Llydaw causeway; 4. Miners' barracks

case with the earliest slates, the copper would be transported by boat down the mountain to Cwm y Glo.

In the second half of the 18th century a woman called Margiad uch Ifan lived in Penllyn. She was a bit of an Amazon, and renowned for her strength and was the chief oarswoman on the boats which brought the ore across the lake. Moreover she built her own boats, would go hunting with the best huntsmen in Snowdonia and could shoe horses. An old Welsh song lists her accomplishments and it is said that she was 102 when she died in 1789.

At the outset, the mine workings were very productive – one miner called Siôn John Roberts spotted a good vein of copper and was able to earn himself £300 in 3 months. Today, the drilling and blasting, the hammering and the milling have come to an end – but there are many kilometres of shafts and huge underground chambers which remain in the mountains as testimony to the industrious nature of these tough old miners.

1. *Copper mining heritage at Sygun; 2. A Padarn copper hauling boat found in the mud of Llyn Padarn*

Sygun Copper Mine

An award winning tourism attraction, Sygun Copper Mine near Beddgelert is a wonderful family experience in Snowdonia – an impressive example of how our industrial heritage can be reclaimed, restored and transformed. Wales was on the copper routes of Bronze Age merchants (2100–750 BC) when the metal was found to be more durable by adding some tin to it. Bronze Age mining began as surface excavations but tunnels were dug to get to the mineral veins deeper in the mountain during Roman times.

In the 17th century a mining commission was set up to develop mining

Sygun Copper Mine tourist attraction

and extraction techniques in the mines. During the Industrial Revolution the demand for copper increased. Sygun Copper Mine and other copper mines in north-western Wales such as Parys Mountain in Amlwch and the Great Orme in Llandudno, were an important source of the metal ore. Electricity increased the demand for copper wires and it was needed to import cheaper copper from abroad. Snowdonia mines couldn't compete and the Sygun mine closed in 1903. After the mine was abandoned stalactites and stalagmites were formed as water trickled through the old tunnels.

Slate quarrying

When the native Welsh princes and nobility lost their power, a new generation of landowners emerged who did not shy from seizing land and riches at every possible opportunity. One of the largest estates in northern Wales was the Faenol Estate. At its zenith, it stretched over 15441ha, encompassing some 27 parishes from the Conwy valley to the Llŷn Peninsula.

The old Welsh family, who were patrons to poets and who maintained vestiges of the old culture, died out and the estate fell into the hands of John Smith from Tedworth, the Speaker of the House of Commons, and subsequently to Thomas Assheton Smith from Cheshire. During the 17th-18th century, the estate was neglected by absentee landlords but it became a little more prosperous when Assheton Smith began opening up slate quarries and stealing the common land (*tir comin*)from the local communities.

The common land had been divided

1. Faenol Estate; 2. Early slate hauling by boat and ponies and carts

between the whole community for over a thousand years under the Welsh laws of Hywel Dda, but Assheton Smith and another landowner insisted on pushing an Enclosure Act through Parliament in their own interests.

There is an old Welsh saying: 'you can be hanged for stealing a sheep from the mountain, but you can be made a lord for stealing the mountain itself,' and this was indeed the case in this area. A number of quarrymen and smallholders who had built cottages on the common land were to be evicted. The squatters organised a meeting which became unruly, and the authorities read out the Riot Act. Without lawyers to fight their case, several of the common land tenants were thrown into Caernarfon gaol. This cleared the way for the landowners to open up the slate quarries.

Quarrying is a very wasteful industry. Ten tons of waste are produced for every ton of slate and more than half the slopes of Elidir Fawr have been scarred by slate works. Two centuries of working the *ponciau* (levels or galleries; sing. *ponc*) has

Old incline walls and slate mills on the Dinorwig Quarry path

thrown up huge spoil tips above the eastern side of Llyn Peris. The quarry shut down suddenly, but not unexpectedly, in 1969.

Slates have been sheared from the rocks of northern Wales for over 1,800 years – slate was used in the Roman fort at Segontium and the Norman castle at Conwy. In the 18th century, slates were mined for private use here, but that was curtailed by Assheton Smith when he enclosed the common land. In 1809, he formed his own company and began to develop the industry on a large scale.

Originally, slates were transported by boat across the lake to Penllyn, Cwm y Glo and from there they were taken in carts to Caernarfon. By 1848–1849, the quarry company had built a railway to transport materials directly from the workshops to the harbour at Felinheli. From there, they would be exported all over the world. Nearly 5,600 tonnes of Dinorwig slate went to Australia in 1882 alone, a year which saw Welsh slate quarries producing over a quarter of a million tons of slate. Slate was utilised in several other ways apart from as a roofing material – gravestones, hearths, billiard tables and telephone switchboards on large ships. But obviously, the greatest demand was for roofing slates – in particular as the Industrial Revolution saw whole new areas being populated almost overnight, and as emigrants established their townships and cities in the New World.

In its heyday, the quarry was a self-sufficient world, with its own barracks to accommodate the workers who would stay there during the week. From Llanberis, you can see the *ponciau* or terraced galleries, which the quarrymen would work, each *ponc* with its own name, such as 'Abyssinia', 'California', 'Twll Mwg' (smoke hole) or 'Aberdaron'.

Working under arduous conditions in all weathers on the rock face, led inevitably to frequent accidents at the quarry, many of which were fatal. In 1860, a hospital was built with its own doctor and operating theatre as part of the quarry. This is now open to the public, showing the beds of the unfortunate inmates and the apparatus used – including a wooden leg which would be lent out to any

1. The 'Blondin' winch at Vivian Quarry;
2. Llanberis quarrymen; 3. Dressed slates at the National Slate Museum

From Dinorwig village, a safe and fenced path winds through the vast quarry

unfortunate amputee until he had purchased his own. A shilling (5p) would be docked from the quarrymen's wages to run the hospital.

Over the years, a number of machines were introduced which facilitated the heavy work, but, to this day, the slate still has to be split by hand. This is a craft which relies on human talent, which, together with the quarrymen's skills and the nature of the rock, ensured that Welsh slates were the very best in the world.

Slate quarrying shelter huts (during rock blasting) and other evidence of the past industry

The Quarry Hospital

In 1860 a quarryman's hospital was built on the slopes above Llyn Padarn. In 1892, Dr R.H. Mills Roberts arrived to take charge of it. During Roberts's period the men organised a 'shilling club'. Under this scheme a shilling was deducted from the wages of each man every week, and in the event of an accident he would be eligible for medical care without any further cost. But the men were expected to pay for medicine and other requirements. This has been described as the first occupational health scheme in Britain and it only came to an end with the foundation of the National Health Service in 1948.

Apart form being compassionate, inspired in his medical achievements and supremely energetic, Mills Roberts was a considerable innovator. He designed metal skull plates and artificial limbs. One of his patients was Edward Jones who lost both arms in a blasting accident. Roberts devised two metal arms to enable him to at least use a knife and fork. Although the hospital was intended primarily for the quarrymen, women and children were eventually treated there as well. The hospital is now a museum where visitors can see photographs on display as well as some of the instruments used by Mills Roberts.

The vastness of the quarry face and the huge efforts of the workforce, all done by hand, has a dramatic effect

National Slate Museum

The work and life of the quarrymen of northern Wales have been preserved and wonderfully presented at the National Slate Museum in Gilfach Ddu in the Padarn Country Park (*Parc Gwledig Padarn*). A good way to begin a visit is to watch the 3D audio-visual film 'Stealing the Mountain', which provides a background and extracts from the history of Dinorwig Quarry and the society which grew up around the slate industry.

The workshop at Gilfach Ddu serviced all the requirements of the quarry, as well as those of the trains and ships. There are over 80km of railway tracks in the quarry itself, not to mention the narrow gauge line down to Felinheli. A visit to the workshops, the machine shop, the smithy and the iron and brass foundry, shows just how self-sufficient the quarry was. The workers used to boast that they could repair anything that a quarry might need – from sharpening a chisel to making a steam engine. A quick tour of the foundry and the template store soon confirms this.

At the National Slate Museum

Every now and then, the foundry is fired and there is an opportunity for visitors to see metal being turned into molten liquid and poured white hot into templates in the beds of sand. Another striking feature in the museum is the big water wheel which supplied power to all the workshops between 1870 and 1925. This was the largest industrial wheel in Wales.

The quarry's main arteries were the inclines which carried the rocks from the different levels. The weight of the full wagons was used to raise the empty wagons back to the top of the slope. You can see craftsmen still engaged in the old craft of splitting (*hollti*) and chipping (*naddu*) in Gilfach Ddu.

In 1998, a terrace of houses from Tanygrisiau near Blaenau Ffestiniog were moved to Gilfach Ddu. Every stone, slate and beam was numbered and subsequently re-erected in their entirety, care being taken with every detail. The houses have now been furnished to convey the three periods in the quarry's history. 1861, the industry's golden age; 1901, the

Craftsmen still display the craft of dressing slates at the museum

time of the strike at the Penrhyn Quarry in Bethesda, a dispute which lasted three years, creating a deep rift in the quarrying community of that town (see the warning in the window 'No scabs in this house.'); the final house in the terrace recreates the atmosphere in 1969, the year Dinorwig Quarry was closed.

The popular 'Caffi'r Ffowntan', which is renowned for its traditional Welsh home cooking, is another attraction to the museum. From the village of Dinorwig, a path has been fenced out offering a dramatic walk through a higher level of the quarry.

Llanberis

Of all the communities within the National Park region, Llanberis probably attracts more guaranteed visitors than any other location.

With the growth of the quarry, a 'new' village was developed at Llanberis. In its heyday, the slate industry employed some 3,000 workers in the region and however hard the work and low the wages might have been, they were much higher than rural wages in general at that time. There was a demand for housing and shops and other services and Llanberis grew to be one of the most important villages in the county. In addition, the tourist industry had begun to establish itself and a number of hotels were built there.

Once again, it was Thomas Assheton Smith who was the first to see the niche in the market for tourism. In 1830, he built the Victoria Hotel on the edge of the village. The road through the Llanberis pass was built in 1831 which made things easier for travellers to access the region. In 1869, the LNWR railway company opened a line from Caernarfon to Llanberis, establishing a station on the site occupied by Electric Mountain (*Mynydd Gwefru*) today.

Although the slate industry produced considerable profits for the owners, very little of that was seen by the quarrymen themselves. Attempts were made during the 19th century to establish a trade union in the north Wales quarries. The quarrymen of Glyn Rhonwy to the north of Llanberis were the first to ensure union recognition by an owner.

In order to prevent trade unionism from spreading any further, the owners tried to stop the quarrymen from meeting – not only in the quarry but also on any piece of land which was owned by the Faenol Estate. At the far end of Llyn Padarn there is a rock which forms a natural amphitheatre standing on the old estate of Lord Newborough of Glynllifon. The quarrymen of the area began to meet in the shadow of the rock and it has become known ever since as 'Craig yr Undeb' (union rock). In 1974, hundreds of people gathered at the rock to celebrate the centenary of the founding of the North

1. 'Craig yr Undeb' – the quarrymen's union meeting place; 2. One of Llanberis' attractive eating places; 3. Victoria Hotel

Wales Quarrymen's Union under the leadership of Robert Parry, Ceunant, and a memorial plaque was put in place to mark the occasion.

Chapels have always been important institutions in the quarrying areas and represent the self-determination of the workers in upholding their own religion. The chapels were also cultural centres running a whole range of musical and literary events which were a feature of the social life in the quarrying communities. *'Hogiau'r eglwys'* (the churchgoers), on the other hand, was a depreciatory term for the quarry stewards – sycophantic officials who crept up to the quarry owners. The Methodist Capel Coch was established at Llanberis in 1777 and although it was rebuilt several times in granite, it kept its original name, the *coch* (red) referring to a much smaller edifice built of brick.

Heritage murals at Llanberis

Beddgelert

The immense popularity of this charming village is not only due to its wonderful setting, but also the myth concerning the hound Gelert. The story has it that Llywelyn Fawr ('the Great') left his hunting dog to guard his baby son while he went out to catch game in the surrounding forest. When he returned he discovered that Gelert's fangs were covered with blood. He was so upset that he was unable to think straight and immediately assumed that the animal had attacked the child. In a fit of fury he plunged his sword into the side of his faithful four-legged companion. But when he went through to the back of his dwelling he discovered the infant asleep in his cot. The dog had killed a wolf to protect the baby, hence the blood. As a result, his life was lived in a state of remorse.

It would seem that this story derives not from the medieval period but from the 18th century. David Pritchard was the first landlord of the Royal Goat Hotel and was anxious to attract visitors to the village. To enable him to fulfil this attempt at early tourist enterprise he enlisted the assistance of two friends and they set about constructing the grave which we see today.

When the Hon. W.R. Spencer visited the area he was very taken by the story of Gelert, which the three village worthies had fabricated and was inspired to write his well-known twenty three verses on the subject. In doing so, he made the village famous beyond the confines of Wales.

Beddgelert stands at the confluence of the Gwynant and the Glaslyn. Within close proximity Aberglaslyn is a delightful location and George Borrow described it as:

> ...wondrous, rivalling for grandeur and beauty anywhere either in the Alps or Pyrenees.

The Beddgelert area is likely to attract those with a serious interest in Arthurian myth. Dinas Emrys (fort of Emrys) is a prominent rocky promontory and, according to Geoffrey of Monmouth's *History of the Kings of Britain*, was given to Merlin by Vortigern, the ruler of Britain at

1. Gelert's grave; 2. Tŷ Isaf; 3. The Goat Hotel; 4. Remembering the hound

some point between AD 400 and 600. Merlin was a poet, astronomer and all manner of other things and was capable of being metamorphosed into a hawk or other living creature.

At the end of the 18th century there is said to have been a ghost at the Royal Goat Hotel. David Pritchard, the landlord, suddenly died without leaving a will. The ghost wandered about the fields, lanes and village frightening everyone except one old labourer. It confronted the labourer in the stables and had a message for Alice, his wife. It instructed the labourer to tell his wife that she would find golden guineas under the hearthstone, two of which she must give to the labourer. This all came to pass and the restless ghost was never seen again.

On a lighter note, Alfred Bestall made his home in Beddgelert. It was he who, for many years, drew the pictures and created the story lines for the Rupert Bear stories in the *Daily Express*. He was the subject of a full-length biography, which appeared in 2003, several years after his death. The book reveals that he was a particularly genial man.

The ashes of the major 20th century Welsh language poet, T.H. Parry-Williams, are buried in the churchyard. His scholarship and literary achievement resulted in his appointment to the Chair of Welsh at the University of Wales at Aberystwyth in 1920.

Many well-constructed and well-maintained footpaths can be found in the area (including the Gwyrfai path from Beddgelert to Rhyd-ddu) and these are enjoyed by the thousands of walkers who walk in the hills each year.

1. *Gelert's grave walk; 2. & 3. The bridge over Colwyn river at the centre of the village*

Capel Curig

Capel Curig is situated on the A5 between Betws-y-coed and Bethesda in the heart of Snowdonia.

At Bryn Gefeiliau (*bryn*: hill; *gefeiliau*: smithies), the Romans had a marching camp – and they had another one at Penygwryd (partly submerged now by the reservoir of the hotel).

In the 19th century Lord Penrhyn was responsible for the building of an inn on the A5 which provided accommodation and refreshment for both coach travellers and pedestrians. The building was enlarged at a later stage and according to one guidebook of the period:

> ...every curious and contemplative observer of the sublimities of nature will certainly be happy in knowing that the very centre of Eryri has been rendered accessible even by carriage.

Plas y Brenin Outdoor Activities Centre was established by the Central

1. Tŷ Hyll, Capel Curig;
2. White water canoeing on the Llugwy river

Council for Physical Recreation and has a considerable reputation for its rock climbing courses.

There is a weather station at Capel Curig and this is the reason why it is quite often mentioned on television weather forecasts in connection with its high levels of rain.

We do not know a great deal about St Curig, but typically of the saints of the Celtic Church, he was a great traveller and many churches, wells and stones are named after him in Brittany. The 15th century bard, Lewis Glyn Cothi, refers to 'the brave knight Curig's coat of mail', which may suggest that at some point he may well have been a soldier.

The original dedication of the church at Capel Curig would have been to Curig Lwyd; at a later date he was displaced by Cyriacus and his mother Julitta, as in other Welsh churches. On account of this confusion, Curig's Festival has been transferred to 16th June.

Curig the Blessed was known as Bishop of Llanbadarn, and his 'cambutta' or upper part of the pastoral staff is described by Giraldus as being 'covered on all sides with gold and silver, and resembling the form of a Cross'.

The church is the smallest in the whole district. The roof is now ceiled internally, showing only the undersides of the principals, which appear to be of the 15th century. This is probably the date of the transept, the old part having been reroofed when the transept was added.

The principal interest of the church rests in the plan. It is the only example in the district in which the double-square plan has not been lengthened in later times.

The bell-turret, doorway, and all the windows are modern, and there are very few mediaeval features left. There is externally a projecting plinth. The brackets at the bottom of the gables are of slate rock and look like 16th-century work. The bell is old, but has no inscription.

There is a curious wooden monumental tablet to the south of the altar, dating back to 1679.

The font, after having served many years for base uses, has been rescued and put into the new church. Judging by its size it belongs to the 15th century, but unfortunately it has been entirely rechiselled.

The churchyard, which was originally very small, has recently been enlarged;

there are no old yew trees.

The chapelry used to belong to, and was kept in repair by, the parish of Llandegai, but was served by the Vicar of Betws-y-coed; and in mediaeval times, both Dolwyddelan and Capel Curig belonged to the Priory of Beddgelert.

On the old road just behind the post office is a farm known as Gelli'r Mynach or 'Gell y mynach' ('monk's grove' or 'monk's cell'), probably also belonging to Beddgelert. The house is now modern, but in 1802 there were said to have been certain wood carvings of mediaeval character internally. The hill behind is known as Cefn y Capel.

The church at Capel Curig

A Snowdon Car Journey

Caernarfon–Beddgelert

Leave Caernarfon following the A4085 towards Beddgelert. At the top of the rise look out on the left for Segontium Roman Fort. The entrance is not all that easy to spot and the small museum looks, at first glance, like a private house, but it is signposted and for anyone interested in archaeology it is a must.

Keep to the A4085, going straight ahead at the next roundabout and in a couple of miles (3.2 km) pass through the village of Waunfawr. Keep on and shortly pass through the hamlet of Betws Garmon to arrive on the banks of Llyn Cwellyn, on the far side of which, the sheer, tree-covered slopes of Mynydd Mawr fall into the water. Halfway along the lake, which supplies water to Caernarfon, there is a car park on the right and opposite, the Snowdon Ranger Youth Hostel.

The next hamlet is Rhyd-ddu where there is excellent parking and toilets on the left, by the current terminus of the Welsh Highland Railway. A little further on down the A4085, with Llyn y Gadair and the Beddgelert Forest on the right, the road continues down hill into the village of Beddgelert. Parking is a little restricted during the height of the season but turning right over the bridge and following the road round there is a car park on the right just before the Goat Hotel.

Beddgelert–Nantgwynant

Leaving the village going south, on the A498, the road follows the banks of the river Glaslyn, dominated on the right by the impressive 2,600 ft (782 m) of Moel Hebog. This is the beautiful Pass of Aberglaslyn, popular with calendar and chocolate box makers! The river was navigable up to Pont Aberglaslyn until William Madocks built his embankment at Porthmadog in the early 1800s to reclaim thousands of acres of land.

Turn left over the bridge on the A4085 and very shortly there is a car park and toilets on the left in the hamlet of Nanmor valley. Leave the main road, and take the minor road on the left through the houses. This attractive road twists and turns, with some short sharp hills until after a mile (1.6 km) it comes to a T-junction by a

Welsh Highland Railway near Rhyd-ddu

Moel Hebog above Beddgelert and Afon Glaslyn at Aberglaslyn

house called Bwlchgwernog. Turn left into what is now the Nanmor valley and follow closely the banks of the river through woods with picnic areas, until after 3 miles (4.8 km) of fairly gentle climbing it emerges into open countryside, with views across the valley on the right to a range of mountains including Cnicht 2,265 ft (689 m), Moel Druman 2,152 ft (676 m) and Ysgafell Wen 2,299 ft (660 m) and in the opposite direction, the Snowdon Horseshoe range.

At the crest of the hill there is a sharp left turn and the road begins to drop down eventually to cross the river Glaslyn onto the A498. Turn right and almost immediately there is a car park and toilets on the right. This is the start of the Watkin Path up Snowdon. The road now starts its steady climb, initially along the shores of Llyn Gwynant and then more steeply to where there are two viewpoints on the left, the higher one giving perhaps the better view of Snowdon. (There is frequently a welcome ice cream van here during the season.)

Nantgwynant–Llanberis

Continue to the top of the hill and take the road on the left, the A4086, by the Penygwryd Hotel. The road climbs up to the Llanberis pass at Pen-y-pass. There is limited parking here and those wishing to stop a while, perhaps to climb Snowdon, would be well advised (particularly in high season) to get here either very early or better still, take one of the Sherpa buses which ply from various points in the Park.

The road down from the pass follows the river Nant Peris, with the flank of Snowdon on the south side and the sheer rock faces of the Glyderau and Y Garn to the north. These rock faces are popular, and at weekends and in season they are crawling with climbers testing their skill. The lay-by on the left is usually full of motorists watching in awe of this seemingly dangerous pastime.

Halfway down the hill just after the bridge, Pont y Gromlech, a large boulder on the right is reputed to have been the abode of an old woman named Hetty while she looked after her sheep and goats. Popular outcry prevented its removal by the authorities in a road-widening scheme! At the foot of the hill is the hamlet of Nant Peris, a centre for campers and climbers, where the only pub is full of these outdoor types in the evening.

The road now follows the shores of

Llyn Peris, veering to avoid Dolbadarn castle before entering the village of Llanberis. There is parking across the road from the Snowdon Mountain Railway terminus, near the National Slate Museum to the right, and limited space overlooking the lake on the village centre by-pass.

Llanberis–Caernarfon

Take the main street rather than the by-pass and halfway along go up Goodman Street on the left (opposite Pete's Eats).

A green May in Nantgwynant

Snowdon and its Villages

Llyn Gwynant and Nantgwynant

After leaving the built-up area the road begins to climb through woods. Breaking out from the trees are the spoil heaps of the vast Glyn Rhonwy Slate Quarry and it is interesting to just stop at the side of the road to get out and look down into the actual quarry. The road climbs more steeply through a series of sharp bends becoming narrow – very narrow in places – unfenced, and with a poor surface, requiring care.

At the top the views are stunning, so find a spot to park and get out. Looking back, down to the left Llanberis and Llyn Padarn, behind which rise the much quarried foothills of Elidir Fawr 3,030 ft (930 m), whilst to the right there is the 'V' of the Llanberis Pass, with the Glyder Fach and Glyder Fawr, both over 3,000 ft (900 m) on the north side of the Pass, and Crib Goch and Yr Wyddfa, again well over 3,000 ft (900 m) on the south side.

Over the cattle grid the road begins to drop down to Bryn Bras Castle passing a reservoir and caravan site on the left and then the outbuildings of the castle itself. Turn right for the A4086 in Llanrug and at the crossroads turn left to follow the main road back to Caernarfon.

Snowdon from the east and Snowdon from Llyn Padarn

Mountain Guides and early travellers

It is said that you can see twenty lakes from the summit of Snowdon on a reasonably clear day. From the summit too, you can see a number of paths stretching like ribbons in the distance – paths which were created by generations of walkers heading for the summit from different directions. It is difficult to believe these days, but in the past, the mountain was devoid of tracks. Then travellers began to show an interest in climbing to the peak which led to the birth of 'Tywyswyr yr Wyddfa' or 'Snowdon Guides'.

Some of the early mountaineers had already experienced the romance of the Alps, and there was a great interest in botany. But without any paths, they had little choice but to hire local men who were familiar with the slopes. They were real characters and dressed in a particular way to attract attention.

One of the most renowned guides was 'Wil Boots' (William Williams, 1805–1861), a boot boy at the Victoria Hotel. He knew the whereabouts of the rare plants and ferns and this, combined with considerable knowledge, led to him becoming known as the 'Botanical Guide' in order to distinguish him from other guides. He accompanied several famous botanists who came to the area looking for

1. 'Wil Boots'; 2. Early mountain guides at Snowdon's summit

plants. He died in an accident on Clogwyn y Garnedd.

Several of the earliest travellers came here because of upheavals in Europe which had placed restrictions on the traditional Grand Tour, but when they reached Snowdonia, the local inhabitants were suspicious of them because they spoke a strange language. They thought they were spies for Napoleon, but their suspicions were allayed somewhat once they understood that the strange gabblings were English and not French!

As the tourist industry flourished, it became a tradition for anyone who came to northern Wales to make an attempt to reach the summit of Snowdon. Trips to the summit on the back of mules and ponies were organised from Llanberis along the more gradual path which leads from the village to the summit.

The Snowdon Horseshoe

A magnificent expedition across the famous Snowdon Horseshoe's highest peaks. Fearsome cliffs. Majestic crags. Lofty arêtes. Classical glacial features. Awesome valleys. Secret lakes. Catapulting streams. Cascading waterfalls. Old miners' road and causeway. One of the great little trains of Wales. Old legend. Romantic panoramas from the highest place in Wales. Glorious environment.

Ascent: about 870 m. Skilfully reinforced paths. Easily followed track. Shattered slopes. Knife-edge ridge crest. Craggy pinnacles. Airy scrambling. Sustained exposure.

Start and finish: At 647556 – Pen y Pass car park; Parking: Car park at the start (fee). Youth hostel near the car park (Tel: 0870 7705990). Café and toilets at the car park. To be attempted only by experienced walkers familiar with exposed rock scrambling.

1st summit: Y Grib Goch 923 m 624551; The mountain walker's ultimate conquest. The breathtaking summit ridge, menacingly exposed throughout, commands the utmost respect. The highest point, in the centre of the ridge, is unmarked and not easily defined. Wales' most hazardous peak.

2nd summit: Crib y Ddysgl 1065 m 610551; The second highest peak in Wales would undoubtedly appeal more to summiteers were it not for its close proximity to Snowdon. It is usually known by its ridge name rather than Carnedd Ugain, the highest point, where there is a trig pillar.

3rd Summit: Yr Wyddfa (Snowdon) 1085 m 609543; The monarch of them all. A Mecca for summiteers from all over the world. The highest mountain in Wales. The summit is crowned by a circular viewing platform surmounted by a trig pillar. A view pointer is displayed on the pillar. About 20 m below the pillar stands Hafod Eryri and the railway station, the upper terminus of the Snowdon Mountain

1. A classic view of the Snowdon horseshoe;
2. Gorffwysfa hostel and restaurant and Pen-y-Pass warden's centre;
3. The car park at Pen-y-Pass

Railway. The new centre replaced the old building complex which was designed in 1935 by Sir Clough Williams-Ellis (architect of Portmeirion) but after years of harsh winters its condition, not surprisingly, had deteriorated. It closed in 2006. The new centre opened in 2009 and is named Hafod Eryri (*hafod*: summer residence of a farming family in Wales). Facilities include a licensed cafeteria, information point and toilets. The centre is open whenever the railway is operating.

4th Summit: Lliwedd 898 m 622533; Possibly the most spectacular precipice in Wales. Great cathedrals of rock plunge sensationally from the crest and one of the finest ridge walks in Europe.

At the west side of the car park, follow the path and pass through the wall gap. Pass beneath the power lines and continue along the reinforced path (known as the Pyg Track). Keep to the well-established path and ascend to the path junction at the pass, Bwlch y Moch, where the south side of the horseshoe comes into view. Turn right off the Pyg Track and follow the rising path towards the towering ridge. Cross the stile at the fence corner and continue up the reinforced path. Follow the path across the scree and scramble up the ridge where there are numerous trails of boot-smoothed rock. On gaining the exposed summit ridge, with an immense abyss to the north, keep near the crest and traverse the 130 m to the first summit, Crib Goch. From here, continue along the ridge crest and progress towards the craggy pinnacled section of the ridge. The pinnacles can be passed by either dropping down to the left and skirting round them or by making a skyline scramble directly over them – either way leading down to the relative comfort of the col, Bwlch Coch. Continue along the ridge path and ascend to the imposing perpendicular slabs at the start of the Ddysgl stretch of the horseshoe. Either drop down to the left and circumvent the slabs or, better still, scramble over them. Continue along the path up the steepening ridge, keep near the crest and ascend to the second summit, Crib y Ddysgl. From here, continue along the path and descend towards the track of the mountain railway at the pass, Bwlch Glas (note the modern standing stone and remember its

Crib Goch with Snowdon rising above it in the background

location). Follow the reinforced path with the railway track to the right and ascend to the third summit, Snowdon.

Descend along Bwlch y Saethau to the twin peaks of Lliwedd and continue round the horseshoe along the blunt rocky shoulder of Lliwedd Bach and then down to join the Miners' Track and back to the car park.

Snowdon summit from Crib Goch

Winter ridge walking is for the experienced

Lliwedd, Bwlch y Saethau and Snowdon

Snowdon Railway

Saturday, 15 December, 1894, was an historical day indeed, for this was the date on which work commenced on building the narrow-gauge railway to the summit of Snowdon. This was the first funicular railway on the island of Britain and the line was opened officially on Easter Monday 1896. It is a remarkable railway journey – 4.7 miles (7.6 km) in length, taking an hour to make the ascent and another hour to come back down, the engine having to travel extremely slowly during the ascent and descent. There were several serious accidents on the line during the early days, but for over a hundred years now, the old train has proved itself to be safer than walking the paths along the high rocky ridges.

With the paths laid down and the train running, the age of the old guides came to an end.

The idea of a railway to the summit of Snowdon was first proposed in 1869, when Llanberis was linked to Caernarfon by the London & North Western Railway. In 1871 a Bill was put before Parliament, applying for powers of compulsory purchase for a railway to the summit, but it was opposed by the local landowner, Mr Assheton-Smith of the Faenol Estate, who thought that a railway would spoil the scenery.

For two decades nothing happened, and Assheton-Smith remained opposed to any plans. However, in 1893 the Rhyd-ddu terminus of the North Wales Narrow Gauge Railways was renamed Snowdon, attracting many of the tourists who previously visited Llanberis and affecting the livelihoods of the accommodation providers who were Assheton-Smith's tenants. After much persuasion Assheton-Smith ultimately gave his assent to the construction of a railway to the summit, and though still the principal landowner in the area, he was not a major influence in the company. However, no Act of Parliament was now required, as the line was built entirely on private land obtained by the company, without any need for the power of compulsory purchase. This was unusual for a passenger-carrying railway, and also meant that the railway did not come under the jurisdiction of the Board of Trade.

The railway was constructed between

Snowdon Mountain Railway

Snowdon and its Villages

December 1894, when the first sod was cut by Enid Assheton-Smith (after whom locomotive No.2 was named), and February 1896, at a total cost of £63,800 (equivalent to £6,658,000 in 2015). By April 1895 the earthworks were 50% complete, a sign of the effort put into the construction work as much as of the lack of major earthworks along much of the route.

The **Snowdon Mountain Railway** (SMR; Welsh: *Rheilffordd yr Wyddfa*) is a narrow-gauge rack and pinion mountain railway in Gwynedd, north-west Wales. It is a tourist railway that travels for 4.7 miles (7.6 km) from Llanberis to the summit of Snowdon, the highest peak in Wales.

The Snowdon Mountain Railway is the only public rack and pinion railway in the British Isles, and after more than 100 years of operation it remains a popular tourist attraction, carrying more than 130,000 passengers annually. The line is owned and operated by Heritage Great Britain plc, operators of several other tourist attractions.

The railway is operated in some harsh weather conditions, with services curtailed from reaching the summit in bad weather and remaining closed during the winter from November to mid-March.

Single carriage trains are pushed up the mountain by either steam locomotives or diesel locomotives. It has also previously used diesel railcars as multiple units.

As part of the Centenary Celebrations the railway held an enthusiasts' weekend in September 1996. This was one of the few occasions when the public were allowed to visit the railway's workshops. Scrap pinion rings were also sold as (rather large) souvenirs. From this time the locomotives were painted in differing liveries, but by 2005 this practice had ended.

Summit building project

In 2006 the Snowdon summit café was demolished and construction of a new visitor centre was started. While this construction was taking place passenger trains terminated at Clogwyn, but the line and a works train was still used to transport workers and materials to the project. On some days, however, the train could not reach the summit and the workers had to walk down to Llechog (Rocky Valley Halt). The new building, Hafod Eryri, was officially opened by First Minister Rhodri Morgan on 12 June 2009.

left: The old summit café;
1. Hafod Eryri; 2. Winter scene; 3. Inside
Hafod Eryri

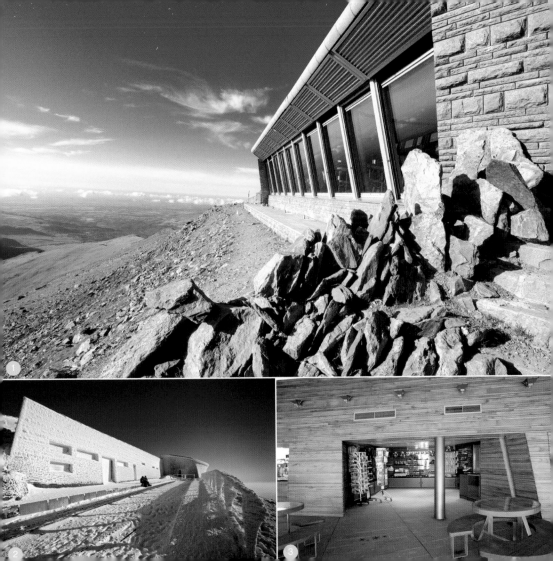

Padarn Railway

The Llanberis Lake Railway runs along part of the trackbed of the defunct Padarn Railway, a 4 ft (1,219 mm) gauge line which connected the quarry with Y Felinheli on the Menai Strait. The Padarn Railway closed in October 1961 and was lifted between 16 May 1962 and February 1963. Following the closure of the Padarn Railway, various plans were made to open a 2 ft (610 mm) gauge tourist railway on the trackbed. The first serious attempt was made by G. Ward a local resident, who proposed a railway that would circle Llyn Padarn using the trackbeds of the British Rail Llanberis branch and the Padarn Railway. This plan would have utilized track and locomotives from the Dinorwic slate quarry, but the company did not pursue the proposal.

In July 1966, a shorter railway running from the quarry company's workshops at Gilfach Ddu near Llanberis to Penllyn was proposed, along the eastern-most three miles of Padarn Railway trackbed. Negotiations were progressing with the company, when in July 1969 the quarry closed at short notice. The quarry's workshops at Gilfach Ddu were purchased by Gwynedd County Council with the intention of creating a Country Park.

In June 1970 the County Council purchased the trackbed of the Padarn Railway and agreed to allow its use for the lake railway.

The Ruston diesel locomotive was quickly put into service laying track. Meanwhile, the first steam locomotive, *Dolbadarn*, was restored to working order. The new railway was built to 1 ft 11½ in (597 mm) narrow-gauge instead of the more unusual 1 ft 10¾ in (578 mm) narrow-gauge used in the quarries. This required all the rolling stock to be regauged, including the locomotives. Tracklaying progressed during 1970 using track recovered from several sources, including some originally used on the Lynton and Barnstaple Railway.

The railway officially opened on 28 May 1971 but because of the need to redesign the carriage stock, the first public trains did not run until 19 July 1971. By the end of the first season, more than 30,000 passengers had been carried. In the winter

1. Padarn Lake Railway station at the village; 2. Alongside the lake; 3. Cei Llydan

of 1971 the railway was extended to its current terminus at Penllyn.

In June 2003 the railway was extended to the town of Llanberis, with a new station close to the start of the Snowdon Mountain Railway. The original terminus at Gilfach Ddu is now a through station serving both the National Slate Museum and the nearby Dolbadarn Castle. On the return journey, passengers may stop off at the Cei Llydan station for a picnic and a chance to enjoy the magnificent views of the Snowdonia mountains above Llanberis pass.

Welsh Highland

The Welsh Highland Railway (WHR) or Rheilffordd Eryri is a 25-mile (40.2 km) long, restored 1 ft 11½ in (597 mm) narrow-gauge heritage railway in the Welsh county of Gwynedd, operating from Caernarfon to Porthmadog, and passing through a number of popular tourist destinations including Beddgelert and the Aberglaslyn Pass. At Porthmadog it connects with the Ffestiniog Railway and to the short Welsh Highland Heritage Railway. In Porthmadog it uses the only mixed gauge flat rail crossing in Wales.

The restoration, which had the civil engineering mainly built by contractors and the track mainly built by volunteers, received a number of awards.

1. Near Llyn Cwellyn; 2. An early WHR engine at Rhyd-ddu; 3. Aberglaslyn

Mountaineering

The Penygwryd Hotel was built in the 1830s and twenty years later, a new hotel was built on the old site of Gorffwysfa Peris at Pen-y-pass. This was the era when experienced scramblers and climbers would come in droves to Snowdonia to tackle the challenging rock faces of Snowdon and Nant Peris. Much pioneering work in mountain craft was undertaken at that time and the names in the visitors' book at the Penygwryd Hotel are a veritable roll call of the top names in mountaineering in Britain during the second half of the 19th century. The owner of the hotel organised a rescue team to search for climbers in distress. This honourable tradition continues.

Among those who have inscribed their names on the ceiling at Penygwryd are John Hunt and Charles Evans and other members of the first expedition to conquer Sargarmatha (Everest) in 1952. The entire team practised and trained here prior to facing the ultimate mountaineering challenge.

Local men also feature among those who developed the craft of conquering the crags. The rector of Llanberis and Llanrug, the Reverend Peter Bayley Williams was a pioneer in this respect, and when the renowned botanist, the Reverend William Bingley came to spend some time with him in 1798, it was this rather unlikely pair who made the the first recorded rock climb. They ascended Clogwyn Du'r Arddu whilst looking for rare alpine plants to plant in the rector's garden! Bingley described the climb: 'without once reflecting on the dangers involved: When he had fixed himself securely to a part of the rock, he took off his belt and holding firmly by one end, gave the other to me... and with a little aid from the stone fairly pulled myself up by it'. According to G.A. Lister, this passage contains the germ of the concept of using a rope for climbing.

The mountains have caught the imagination of a large number of writers, artists, photographers and climbers. The tendency of some of the Victorian travellers, however, was to view the country as a personal playground, and their scribblings betray ignorance and

1. The climber's logo on the Penygwryd Hotel sign; 2. Mountaineering memorabilia at the hotel; 3. Clogwyn Du'r Arddu

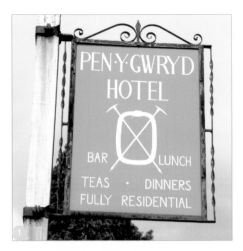

inexperience. The mountains can be very dangerous where the weather changes rapidly.

Today, however, there are plenty of opportunities to appreciate the risks involved and to learn how to avoid them, with information updates on the weather on the peaks available at the Llanberis Visitor Centre. The first National Park in Britain was established in Snowdonia in 1951, and gradually visitors have come to learn that it is not a park in the sense of somewhere to play in. Shepherds still go about their ancient craft on these mountains and the old way of life is protected here, just as much as the magnificent scenery. The beauty of Snowdonia would not be as it is today were it not for the community which has lived on its shores, river valleys and slopes for thousands of years. The crafts and the natural conservation which have been part and parcel of the farming communities have shaped and created the character of this part of the world. The Park now recognises that the intrinsic beauty of Snowdonia cannot continue without the support and the continued existence of the local community, and natural conservation is seen to go hand in hand with the protection of the rights of a Welsh-speaking community and its inherent culture.

As well as respecting paths and not leaving litter, the modern visitor has also learnt – in contrast to the old rector of Llanberis – that wild flowers look better in their natural habitat than in cultivated gardens!

1. Nant Peris; 2. Fine climbing rocks above Nant Peris; 3. Old boots at Penygwryd Hotel

Sunset behind Snowdon

The majesty of the climb

Electricity

The legendary giants and fairies of legend are not thin on the ground around Llanberis, but having visited Electric Mountain (*Mynydd Gwefru*), the visitor can really claim to have come face to face with a giant! This is the largest electricity pump-storage station in Europe, mostly hidden in the core of Elidir Fawr with the station itself located in the biggest man-made cavern in the world.

In creating this power station, the upper lake – Llyn Peris – was totally drained, so it could be deepened and enlarged. The lake contained the *torgoch*, a unique species of fish, which has remained unchanged since the last Ice Age. The fish were carefully netted and transported to other deep lakes in Snowdonia. Marchlyn Mawr high up on the slopes of Elidir was also enlarged. The water comes down from Marchlyn Mawr to turn the turbines in the mountain before being discharged into Llyn Peris. Then the same water is pumped back up to Marchlyn Mawr to await the next urgent demand for electricity on the National Grid.

Although the power station is in the heart of the mountain under the old quarry, you can go in to see it and to wonder at the incredible feat of engineering which has made it possible.

The visit begins in the Electric Mountain centre on the shores of Llyn Padarn near Llanberis. Here the technology is explained and there is an opportunity for children to get hands-on experience of producing their own electricity. Care has been taken to provide access and facilities for the disabled, in the building and throughout the tour. A minibus will then take the party, accompanied by a guide, deep into the mountain to give them a taste of the 16 km of tunnels and the extraordinary engineering involved.

When Llyn Peris was drained, an old clinker boat from the 16th century emerged from its depths. It had been lying in the silt on the bottom of the lake for 500 years. The boat was restored and, together with a dugout canoe from the 12th century, is displayed in a special room in the

1. Electric Mountain (Mynydd Gwefru) *visitor centre at Llanberis with its café (2) and galleries (3)*

1. *Marchlyn Mawr, high on Elidir Fawr;*
2. *Huge water tunnels inside the mountain;*
3. *The electricity turbines;*
4. *The power station near Llyn Peris*

Electric Mountain museum.

Supernatural legends are not just from the past in this area. Whilst work was being done on Marchlyn Mawr, a new folk legend sprang up. One day, some workers saw a huge dumper truck, with two men

on board, slipping backwards into the lake and disappearing into the depths. Two men on the shore were quick-witted enough to leap into a boat in an attempt to save their fellow workers, but there was no sign of them. Suddenly, a huge gust of wind swept over the waters of the lake. The men were sucked out of the lorry and deposited in the boat!

It is not surprising in an area which is so renowned for its legends, that new ones are still being created. Whether you believe them or not, the 'giant' still roars in Snowdonia and illuminates the land with his awesome lightning.

Another part of the complex electricity scheme

A view of the power station from Dinorwig Quarry

Tourism & attractions

Today, Padarn Country Park (*Parc Gwledig Padarn*) on the shores of Llyn Padarn offers a range of facilities and attractions amidst some of the most dramatic scenery in Snowdonia.

There are a number of theme trails which can be followed in the area. Llwybrau Llechi ('the slate trails') cut across the valley floor and lower slopes and follow in the footsteps of the old quarrymen as they made their way back and forth to work in all weathers. There are also paths which have been adapted for the disabled and for cyclists. The park itself extends over some 325 ha, and contains two Sites of Special Scientific Interest – Coed Allt Wen and Llyn Padarn – as well as a local Nature Conservancy site. For those who enjoy a leisurely stroll, there is Llwybr Glas y Dorlan ('the kingfisher trail'), which leads from the main car park along the edge of the lake and this path has also been adapted for wheelchairs and pushchairs.

The Vivian Quarry also provides a chance to do some rock-climbing with ropes or to plumb the depths with diving gear. From here you can also visit the only incline in Wales which has been fully restored and is operational once more. Small sailing and rowing boats can be hired on the lake, or you can enjoy the scenery on board *Brenhines Eryri* and hear stories from the area's history.

In 1848, the owners of the Dinorwig Quarry built the narrow-gauge railway for the quarry's use. Nowadays, the old locomotives still puff their way valiantly along the rails. Once again, the views from the train cannot be seen from the car. On the return journey, the train stops at Cei Llydan. The passengers can get out and wander the woods at Fachwen and enjoy a quiet picnic or the adventure park facilities, before catching a later train back.

There are plenty of eating houses and cafés in the area – the National Slate Museum, Llyn Padarn railway, Electric Mountain and the railway to the summit of Snowdon all have good food and drink facilities and there are several cafés and restaurants in the village offering high quality refreshments. The village streets

1. The heritage railway passing through Padarn Country Park; 2. Pleasure boat on Llyn Padarn; 3. The 'geat incline' at the park

offer a range of shops and exhibitions for those who are looking for crafts and souvenirs of their visit to Llanberis. There are several slate craftsmen in the area – some of them ex-quarrymen, their skill in carving this hard rock into clocks, fans, garden sculpture or house name plates a constant source of admiration. There are quite a few local potteries too – some of which are open to the public – and jewellery makers, coppersmiths, artists, picture framers and reproduction print manufacturers, all provide entertaining displays and an opportunity to buy interesting and varied wares. All in all, a taste of the unique landscape and heritage of Llanberis will enrich your experience of Wales (see www.visitsnowdonia.info).

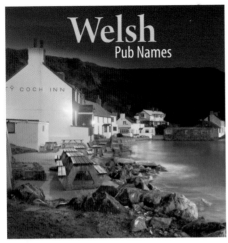

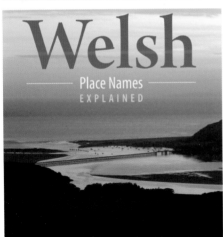

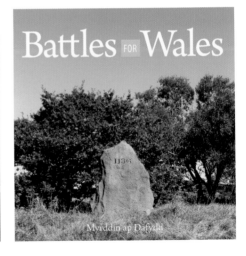